T0380916

Go forth and change the world.

ISBN: Softcover   978-1-7960-2265-0
       Hardcover   978-1-7960-2266-7
       EBook   978-1-7960-2264-3

Print information available on the last page.

Rev. date: 03/23/2019

To order additional copies of this book, contact:
Xlibris
1-888-795-4274
www.Xlibris.com
Orders@Xlibris.com

A Night in the Albornian Forest is 14 year old author Mahati Varanasi's debut book. Mahati is a freshman at Monta Vista High School in Cupertino, California. Mahati's passion for writing comes from her personal penchant to enact social change and create meaningful plots out of everyday situations. Her goal in writing this book is to inform young children about the effects of global warming on animals and humans. Mahati hopes that this book will be the first in a series that teaches young children about real problems and how they can contribute in making the world a better place.

A Night in the Albornian Forest

Deep in the forest of
Albornia, night started to
fall.

Next to the forest was the small village of Carlin. In the village lived the most feared inhabitants of Albornia, Man!

" the specter
of man is a
frightening
shadow
casting its dark
on all that
comes near it. "

Man found joy in
pulverizing and plundering
the plentiful resources of
Albornia. Man was
wasteful. He was dangerous
to the land and all the
animals who lived there.

Man's favorite sport was hunting. Once a year, the entire village of Carlin would march into the forest with their guns and knives to hunt the animals. Some they took back to eat, but most often, they would leave the rotting carcass of the fallen animal on the forest floor to be picked at by the vultures.

"man will pilfer and he will take. He will take until the land has nothing more to give."

He cut down trees, wasted
water, and polluted the air
to build his big towers.
Albornia couldn't go on like
this much longer. The
temperature would
increase, drought would
prevail, the animals would
leave, and the fertile land
and all its trees would
wither and die.

The animals knew that they had to put a stop to this destruction. King Leon, the lion king of the forest summoned all animals to a meeting at the Banyan tree in the middle of the night, when the humans were asleep.

"We must find a way to tame the humans. Our land cannot survive like this much longer. Yes, Owl?"

"Your Majesty, instead of waging war with the humans, we should find a way to compromise with them. Let us write a treaty that divides this land and its resources evenly and fairly amongst us."

"Good idea, Owl. Please get to writing the treaty. Be ready to present it at our next meeting in 2 days."

two days later

"there exists no enemy that cannot be overcome."

"King Leon, I have written the treaty. Would you like to hear it?"
"Most certainly, Owl."

"'Man, for the past 5 years, our species have lived on the same land, but we have not been co-habitants. You have watched us starve and die while you waste our valuable resources. Our civilization, and ultimately yours, will not be able to go on like this much longer. We must reach a compromise to save our shared home. Our idea for such a compromise is this - We each take resources exactly in the amount needed for our survival. We don't waste. For every tree you chop down, you must plant 3 new ones. The most important of all, you must discontinue your yearly hunt of the animals in this forest. We don't enter your village, and in return, you don't come to our forest.'"

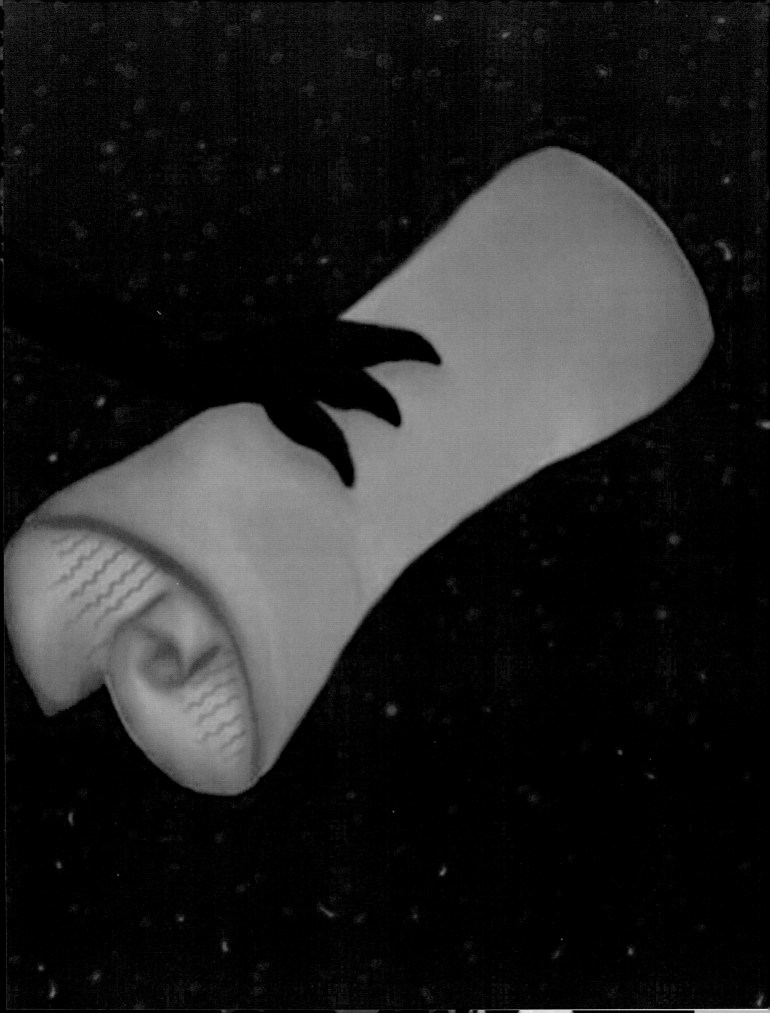

"Well said Owl, very well said. I shall take the treaty into the Village of Carlin at dawn tomorrow."

"never settle for unhappiness. always strive for harmony."

As King Leon said, he took the treaty and walked into the Village of Carlin at the crack of dawn to meet the Chief of the Village, Chief Ferdinand.

"King Leon, what brings you to our village?"

"Chief, I have brought with me a treaty to finally initiate peace between our two communities."

"Well then, let us hear it."

King Leon read the Chief
the treaty. The Chief was
silent for a moment and
looked at the ground. When
he looked up again, he had
tears in his eyes.

"On behalf of the Village of Carlin, I accept the terms of this treaty on the condition of one change, we live not only in peace, but we live as friends. We don't stay away from each other, we stay with each other. We stay together."

At these words, King Leon was overwhelmed with happiness.

"By all means, Chief."

Never again in the history of Albornia did any conflict arise. The land stayed green. The resources stayed plentiful. Everything was peaceful.

Deep in the forests of Albornia lives a large variety of animal species, but their numbers are slowly and tragically dwindling. The reason? Man. On the outskirts of the forest lives the biggest threat the animals have ever faced. With man and the animals at war, it is up to the leaders of the two communities to make peace, and save their lands from destruction.

Printed in the United States
By Bookmasters